Interior Designs

A play

Jimmie Chinn

Samuel French—London
New York-Toronto-Hollywood

INTERIOR DESIGNS

First presented at the Duke's Head, Richmond, Surrey, on 6th April, 1987, under the title *Three Into One,* with the following cast of characters:

Him	Michael C. Brazier
Holly	Jackie Abbey-Taylor
Amy	Fiz Marcus
Irene	Sally Campbell

Directed by Judi Lamb

Time—the present

COPYRIGHT INFORMATION
(See also page ii)

To Pat and Vera and their lovely
"Duke's Head"

Other plays by Jimmie Chinn published by
Samuel French Ltd

After September
Albert Make Us Laugh
But Yesterday
From Here to the Library
Home Before Dark
In By The Half
In Room Five Hundred and Four
Pity About Kitty
A Respectable Funeral
Something To Remember You By
Straight and Narrow
Sylvia's Wedding
Take Away the Lady
Too Long An Autumn

INTERIOR DESIGNS

A bare stage

A folded stepladder and a paintbrush at one side; four chairs

The stage is imaginatively lit

Him, Amy, Holly and Irene are sitting, each in a separate area of light

Amy I didn't know he was married. (*She pauses*) He never said.
Holly He never said he was married—*I* didn't know.
Irene He said he was married—but he wasn't—I could tell.
Amy He *never* said he was married!
Him (*with a smile*) Well—I wouldn't would I? I ask you.
Amy It was a Tuesday. I'll always remember. Tuesday... Now, to tell the truth I'm not a lover of Tuesdays. Never was—don't know what it is—goes back to childhood, I think. We always had sago on a Tuesday—you know—school dinners an' that. So, being as I hated sago I also hated Tuesday 'cos that was the day we had it on see ... and ever since I've had a real dislike of Tuesdays. (*She pauses*) Why am I telling you all this? Oh, yes—that's why I recall the incident so well. "Odd jobs", he says.
Him (*calling out into the audience*) Odd jobs?
Amy (*calling over to him*) What about 'em?
Him Are you thick or what? Odd jobs—about the house—I do 'em. About the house an' that.
Amy (*to the audience*) Well—I mean—when you're on your own an' that—you often need a helping hand—you know—putting up shelves an' that.

Him (*calling out*) I do 'em proper. I'm not a wanker if that's what you're thinking, bleedin' good job *I* do. Proper screws with rawlplugs, rounded corners for maximum protection. Nothing shoddy; my own screwdrivers—the lot—*and* cheap!

Amy "Do you know the work of Visconti?", he said over a cup of tea. So I knew he was cultured an' that, well-read an' that. I mean—when a casual odd-job bloke starts on about Visconti you *know*—don't you? You know he's not a wanker an' that.

Irene Of course I knew who Visconti was—but I could tell he didn't. He drank his tea and there was a pause.

Him *Death In Venice*—that was great; powerful and not as some might think about poofs… Far from it.

Amy I didn't know what he was on about. "I've got a couple of shelves you can do", I said. "In the bathroom they need doing", I said. "Have you got your implements with you?", I said.

Him Implements?

Amy Tools?

Him I wouldn't be offering to do your odd jobs if I didn't have tools—now would I? What do you take me for? (*He pauses*) Keep falling down do they?

Amy (*calling over to him*) What?

Him Your shelves! (*To the audience*) What have I got here? ~~B re~~

Holly I read the news on TV-am, that's obviously why you know my face. I get it all the time—in the street—in shops. I can be filling my trolley in Tesco's and a complete stranger will say "Don't I know that face?" I'm used to it.

Him (*calling out into the audience*) Don't I know that face? *Desert Island Discs*?

Amy Now, sex was the furthest thing from my mind—I mean—I was only too glad to have my nice bathroom shelves done proper, and he seemed nice enough… And he never said he was married. (*She pauses*) And I never asked.

Holly I'm up in the mornings you see. Early. Very early. Extremely early as a matter of fact. On the air by five a.m. Fresh and breezy—smelling of Badedas and coffee. That's where he must have seen me.

Him (*smiling*) 'Ere—don't I know that face?

Irene "Do you wallpaper?", I asked. "I'm in need of a man to hang my wallpaper", I said, "nothing flashy—no five-hundred pound job—a simple, everyday wallpaper job". That's what I said.

Amy And then—after he'd finished the shelves—and I *was* very pleased with them—I said "What about a wallpaper job", I said. "My hall", I said, "it needs a bit of wallpaper—what with Christmas coming", I said. Honest—I wish I'd kept my mouth shut.

Holly He moved in on the Wednesday before my birthday and stayed—oh, several months—on and off. But he never said he was married.

Him (*going to Irene*) You've got to prepare Miss——?

Irene (*a little warily*) Tyson. Miss Irene Tyson.

Him You've *got* to prepare, Miss Tyson. Preparation is the secret: strip off the old paper—see—sand down the surfaces, fill in the old cracks with Polyfilla—I can get it cost price—paint all the woodwork *before* you stick up the paper. Oh, yes, preparation is the secret at all times.

Irene How much?

Him and Irene freeze

Amy *He*'d gone, pissed off—Jack I mean. He was last seen in Brent Cross market with her—what's-she-called? I was better off without him—mind—oh, my God, yes, much better off... Unreliable—always was—very, very unreliable. He'd had other tarts since the day we married—I knew all that. Right sod he was, but I missed his knowledge of Do-It-Yourself, see. I can manage without all the other—screwing an' that—but you're lost if your shelves keep falling down—aren't you? I mean! That's why I was glad of *him*. *And* he carried his own screwdrivers an' that—Jack had taken everything, see... Oh, yes... Left the soddin' kids but took his tool kit. I ask you—I was left wasn't I?—helpless.

Him and Irene unfreeze

Him (*to Irene*) You need a man about the house, Miss. A real man.

Amy "You need a man about the house", he said. "I know that", I said, "you find me one", I said.

Irene How much? I'm a teacher. I'm afraid I don't earn a fortune.

Him Poor cow.

Amy (*resentfully*) Who?

Him (*turning away from Irene and calling over to Amy*) You!

Holly I'd moved in during the summer—July actually—I was attracted to the house as soon as I saw it—the trees and everything. I'd always dreamed of living in a street with trees, I adore them—I really do. Elms, oaks, the ash—I was literally surrounded by them—and the garden: a little large perhaps, but manageable, that's also what attracted me, and it has a tall fence, all round.

During the following, Him puts on a pair of glasses and brings out a copy of The Times

So the privacy was very appealing; I suppose that's what finally decided me. I said to Nigel...

He turns round to face the audience and opens his newspaper

Nigel, I said...

Him (*as Nigel, reading his paper with no interest in her*) Sorry dear...?

Holly We need look no further—paradise is here—within our grasp.

Him What, dear...?

Holly (*to the audience*) It was obvious he wasn't so keen—but I know why now, don't I? Nigel had other fish to fry. (*To him*) The house, Nigel—it's perfect.

Him It's okay, I suppose. Bit big, surely?

Holly It's super, Nigel ... just what we need.

Him Is it...?

Holly (*slightly irritated*) Of course.

Him I don't know why you want to move anyway. The flat at Redcliffe Manor suits us fine.

Holly But it's rented. We need to look to the future. Our future. (*She
   pauses, then looks across at him*) You do love me, don't you?
Him Don't be silly, darling.

*He walks away into the darkness, and, unnoticed by the audience,
discards his glasses and the newspaper, puts a long college scarf
round his neck and picks up a box of Scrabble*

Holly (*to the audience*) He was happy with the flat because it was
   rented—but the house—oh, God, no! Too much of a commit-
   ment, you see—much too long term for him. Of course I should
   have known—I should have guessed when I found the letter in his
   pocket ... it was from *her*. "That's all over", he'd said to me ...
   but obviously it wasn't. Still, there you are—don't tell me—love
   is blind and all that nonsense...
Irene (*to the audience*) Love...? I've never really known it I
   suppose. But then what you've never had you never miss. Of
   course there was Cecil...

*Him turns round, now Cecil, and comes to stand beside Irene,
Scrabble in hand*

   Cecil Coke at school. I suspect he's sort of "in love" with me ...
   but honestly—have you *seen* him...?
Him (*now Cecil*) Hallo, Miss Tyson—how about it?
Irene He's quite nice—but such a bore. And everything—
   absolutely everything—has to have a *double entendre*...
Him How about it? Fancy a session or what? On the table—eh?
   Over lunch...?
Irene (*weary of him*) What is it, Cecil?
Him (*with a silly laugh*) Scrabble, of course. What else did you
   think I meant...?

*She raises her eyes to heaven, takes the box of Scrabble from him;
he again walks away out of the light, removes the scarf, and puts on
a pair of paint-stained overalls*

Irene (*to the audience*) And what's the use of playing Scrabble with someone who can't even spell? All right—call me selfish—maybe I am—but I don't need a man. I'm perfectly content the way I am. I know Cecil would marry me tomorrow—but what would be the point? The only difference would be that we'd play Scrabble in bed! (*She pauses*) Then of course—I met *him*!

Holly And then of course ... I met *him* ... what's-his-name. He'd obviously recognized me from the television...

Him walks into her light, still putting on his overalls, ready to start work

Him 'Ere... don't I know that face...?

Holly Honestly, it does have its compensations being famous—restaurants, theatres, etc.—but, my *God*, it can have its drawbacks. But there you are. And of course, I needed help. I was stranded, wasn't I? High and dry. I mean—the house was very attractive but parts of it were falling down...

Him Falling down is it...?

Holly (*not hearing this*) It needed to be completely rewired. Central heating—how anybody can *live* without that! New plumbing, and the ceiling in the little conservatory was awfully cracked—and there was I—helpless.

Him (*to Holly*) I can do all that for you. I'm very versatile, Miss——

Holly Masterson. Holly Masterson. Perhaps you know my face. (*To the audience*) I *was* wary at first—you know how one is—indeed how one *must* be in this day and age... But he seemed genuine, I loved his disarming manner. All right, so he was a little bit—well—but he was quite attractive, in his way. Yes?

Him (*to the audience with a smile*) Yeah. Well.

Holly But he never said he was married. I mean—life had been complicated enough by Nigel—all I needed was my bits doing.

Him (*to Amy*) Going to take a bit longer—wallpapering your hall—specially if you want it done by Christmas. I mean—a couple of shelves in a bathroom—takes no time at all—but your actual wallpaper takes much longer. There's all the preparation see—stripping off, sanding down, filling in, lining up, clearing away—that all takes time. And I like to do a proper job—nothing shoddy—nothing second rate. That's why I'm in such demand you see, odd-job men are in very great demand in this day and age—see? You know Holly Masterson? Reads the news an' that? Well, I've been doing a lot of work for her just lately and she's more than satisfied. And Miss Irene Tyson, school mistress in Argyle Place? She's crying out for me to tile her kitchen—and *she* works to a very tight budget—but that's the beauty see... Moving as I do in the right circles I can get most things at cost, except your actual carpet—now if you want carpet you'll have to pay full price see—'cos I'm not familiar with anyone in the trade. Married? Not likely. I'm a free agent see—come and go as I please—that's the beauty.

Holly I thought it would be simpler if he moved in—no waiting around for him to turn up.

Him (*to Amy*) I can be available twenty-four hours a day Mrs——

Amy Tappley, but you'd best call me Amy. I don't care to be reminded of the Tappleys.

Him Elsewhere is he? I understand, Amy, I fully understand. I find that for most of the ladies I do for the man in their life has left home—leaving them helpless an' that.

Amy exits

Holly (*calling across to him*) Are you married, Mr——?

Him Good God, no! Couldn't be doing with all the fuss. I'm a free agent—yes, I can move in—seems the wisest thing... The little room? Overlooking the back garden? That'll do me. Just a place to lay my weary head—that's all I need. Shall we say Wednesday? I'll be round with my bits and pieces. A cup of Nescafé and a couple of biscuits—that'll do me.

Irene To tell the truth—I thought he was simple-minded.

Irene exits

Holly goes to a darkened area

Him gets a stepladder, sets it up and climbs it, paintbrush in hand, and starts "painting"

Amy enters carrying a cup of coffee for Him

Amy Coffee then. You never stop do you? I mean—I've got to say I'm more than pleased with the progress—I mean, three weeks and you've put up shelves, done my hall, cleared my drains and now—here you are—in my bedroom. Yes, I'm more than pleased… Coffee then?

Him Put it down there will you—I hate to stop in the middle of a cornice. I told you I was good—didn't I?

Amy You did. An' I've got to admit I didn't believe you—and so cheap. You see I've been let down by men once too often—you get very, very wary.

Him (*involved with the painting*) As you can see—I'm picking out the cornice a lighter shade of yellow—Primrose Blush it's known as in the trade—they mix it for me special—they've got a machine an' that.

Amy (*not listening*) I married him when I was only seventeen—seventeen! I ask you. It's nothing is it? And I knew then that he wasn't to be trusted. I found him in the back of a furniture van screwing the life out of Muriel Dawlish—my best friend she was—or so I thought… Knickers round her ankles—skirt up past her handbag—knocking off my husband and we'd only been married three days. We was moving into the flat in Bakerlite Dwellings—number nineteen it was—he'd hired a van and she was helping us. I couldn't lift, see, seeing as I was seven months gone with Adrien… So she'd said, "Don't worry, Amy", she said, "I'll be round, half-past ten", she said, "to put up your heavies an' that". Soddin' little whore… All the time she had her eye on Jack, and he on her—see what I mean? He on her.

Him You don't half rabbit on, you're giving me a soddin' headache here. Do you like the cornice? Primrose Blush? Nice in'it?

Amy (*not listening*) Seventeen! I mean—you know nothing at that age do you? It's terrible being a woman really. Men! They take bleedin' advantage don't they? (*She looks up to him*) Here—you don't even make a mess, do you? Wouldn't even know you'd been here. I'm in the kitchen if you need me.

Amy exits into the darkness beyond the light

Irene enters with a cup of coffee and joins Him at the foot of the ladder

Irene And the summers seemed longer then, autumn was always far away and winter unheard of. We were young of course and everything is timeless when you're young, but we were carefree, Mr——. Carefree, light-hearted, and gay.

Him (*busily painting*) Gay was you? It's called Primrose Blush... Like it do you?

Irene (*not listening*) Everything's changed—I suppose it must—life must go on, but it's never the same. I went to college in Dingleworth—no-one's ever heard of it... Dingleworth? they say, Where's that? Oh, but it was beautiful, nestled in the Cheviots, by Swanstone Manor and Pendlecrest, by the River Creen... You'd know it if I pointed it out on the atlas—lush green countryside, unspoilt by the cruelty of man—I got a degree, in needlework and craft, but I've never taught it. Strange, isn't it, how fate takes a hand? (*Looking up*) I thought you were doing everything white?

Him Well—yes—but I thought a touch of Primrose Blush on the cornice might add a touch of called-for class... Don't you like it?

Irene I suppose I do really—as you say it puts it above the commonplace.

Him Where's Dingleworth?

Irene (*laughing*) I knew you'd ask—everyone does—it's snuggled at the foot of the Cheviots ... you know Swanstone Manor?

Him (*working*) Oh yeah...

Irene And Pendlecrest—the Creen?

Him (*not knowing at all*) Oh yeah!

Irene Well—there. Heavenly really. But I've never been back. (*Looking up*) You know I do like it. Perhaps you could move into my bedroom next, Mr——er?

Holly calls from the darkness

Louder

Holly Avocados. Do you like them?

Irene (*moving away into the darkness*) Who knows ... one day perhaps I might return there.

Irene exits

Him (*calling to Holly*) What?

Holly joins Him at the foot of the ladder

Holly Avocados—do you like them? I thought we'd have them with dinner this evening—if you like them that is.

Him I can manage to feed myself, Holly—you have enough to do.

Holly Nonsense. I have to cook for myself so I may as well cook for you. Some wretched woman recognised me in Sainsbury's today . . . it can be very tiresome you know. (*Looking up*) What on earth's that?

Him What?

Holly That ghastly colour for God's sake—it's yellow.

Him I thought it added a touch of distinction—just the cornice—no?

Holly No. Certainly not! It looks frightful, just keep everything apple-white as we arranged—otherwise I'll think you're taking liberties.

Him (*taking offence*) Oh, well—if that's how you feel. . . (*He sits on the ladder*)

Holly Oh, come along now—you're surely not taking offence?

Him Yes, I bloody well am taking offence! Are you suggesting I have no taste?

Holly Now I'm not suggesting that at all. I simply said. . .

Him There's me wanting to add just a little touch of artistic licence—and there's you being friggin' insulting.

Holly I'm sorry. Look, I really am sorry—my mind's so full of work and everything—look, forgive me, I wouldn't upset you for the world—now would I? I value your help too highly. . . Please—please say you forgive me. No?

Him Shall I paint over this then—the Primrose?

Holly You'll do nothing of the kind I love it—as you say it . . . it. . .

Him Places it above the commonplace?

Holly Exactly. Dinner? Sixish?

Him (*starting work again*) Yeah—fine. Oh, by the way. . .

Holly Yes?
Him I don't like avocados. Keep the meals simple will you.
Holly Of course.
Him And that sauce you served last night with the lamb? I prefer gravy.
Holly Yes, dear.

Holly exits into the darkness

Him (*to the audience as he works*) You gotta be very firm with these women—specially if they're on their own an' that—they can be bossy given half the chance, you know, try to take over an' that ... the way they do ... but you have to be very firm, put your foot down right at the start—otherwise ... well, Gawd knows where you'd end up—*and* never go to bed with 'em on the *first* day—hold it in abeyance. Mark my words it's the best thing. I quite like this cornice. (*He carries on "painting"*)

enter

Amy, Holly and Irene enter and stand in their own light each with a mug of coffee in hand

Amy (*to the audience*) I thought I'd be lonely—lost—but I'm not really. I love the independence.
Holly I love the independence. I do—I love it.
Irene I love being alone—the independence—I love it.
Amy He knocked me about—was rude—filthy-minded ... well, I ask you, who the hell wants all that?
Holly Nigel was fine—I mean—we all have our faults and I'm sure I can be very difficult to live with—all the fuss I get whenever we're out—people recognizing me everywhere I go—but I can't help that can I? No, Nigel was fine if everything was going *his* way.
Amy I mean, men are fine if everything's going their way—but when you boil it down, who needs them? And when you've had all of *that*—well—it's nice to give it a rest isn't it? You know, I haven't read a book in fifteen years—I haven't—not since I left school have I ever read a book—I haven't looked at pictures—

listened to music—been for a walk by the river for Christ's sake—and it's only down the bottom of my street... But would I dream of going? No—because it wasn't expected of me—see. I had the kids—his mother till she snuffed it—chasing about like a blue-arsed fly. I ask you...

Holly I'm career-minded—always have been—and terribly, terribly single-minded ... as I said—independent—and with a job like mine—my goodness—I have to be all those things—I can't have hangers-on can I? And whichever way you look at it—Nigel *was* just that: a very well-built hanger-on.

Irene I'm a solitary person—always have been—not lonely, mind—never that—but solitary, independent, "a loner" my father used to say... "Irene's a loner, Mother", he used to say ... and, of course, he was right. Who needs people? I have my little house, the garden, the cat, my job—I could do without that but one needs the money—church on Sunday, a walk by the river after lunch at weekends, my books, the needle-work ... and I paint—sometimes—not these days because life is very hectic at the moment... but one day ... one day I'll be glad of it again. As I say, who needs people? Especially men. But everyone thinks you're strange if you haven't got a "man friend", and yet they do nothing but gossip if you do—especially other teachers, believe me—teachers are the worst for gossip ... it's because they lead such crashingly dull lives I suppose. They think I'm carrying on with Cecil Coke in Maths, but I ask you. Cecil Coke of all people, I mean—I do play Scrabble with him at lunchtime—but as for anything else... (*Pause*) I did have a boy friend ... at Dingleworth. "Where's that?", I hear you cry... Well it was Teacher Training near Swanstone Manor, but, honestly—that didn't last long. I much prefer the company of women ... and I don't mean ... there you are you see ... one has to explain nowadays. It never used to be like that, did it? It's quite simply, well, I can do without men—I prefer the independence.

Amy No—the independence—I love it...

Holly No—I much prefer it...

Irene No—it's much the wisest thing...

Amy Feet up ... watch the telly ... nice love story...

Holly In bed ... alone ... with a nice book...
Irene I've managed without men up until now—so really...
Amy (*offering the mug of coffee up to Him*) Coffee, love?
Holly (*doing the same*) Coffee, darling?
Irene (*doing the same*) Coffee, Mr ... er——?
Him (*busy working*) I might do one wall in this—should look nice...

Black-out

A pool of light comes up around the stepladder. Him sits on it (top step perhaps)

Amy (*coming into the light*) Jack. Jack.
Him (*now Jack*) Yeah?
Amy Jack, you remember Muriel Dawlish?
Him (*distantly*) Who?
Amy Dawlish ... Muriel ... Muriel Dawlish—the back of the furniture van—you remember.
Him Why her? Why now?
Amy We never talk about that do we?
Him Why should we?
Amy It came as a terrible shock to me that.

Amy doesn't get any answer, so she sits on the lower step of the ladder

   Jack?
Him No sense of humour that's your trouble, Amy.
Amy And Sylvia Shotter ... Rita Mapp ... Gloria Thompson... (*She looks up at him*) Enid Whitely?
Him (*indignantly*) I never had Enid Whitely. Where did you get *that* story from?
Amy I'm sorry—I thought...
Him You wanna watch your mouth, girl. That can get you into trouble that can. Who told you I'd had Enid Whitely? Come on—who told you?

Amy I just thought…

Him Jessica Salt, right? Jessica-big-mouth-Salt? Right?

Amy Well…

Him She wants to watch her great big ugly mouth. Well, she's got it wrong, see. I never went to bed with Enid Whitely so that's that.

Amy You never went to bed with Muriel Dawlish—you had her in the back of the van.

Him What is all this, Amy? Bleedin' inquisition time. Why drag all that up? You're happy now—aren't you?

Amy Well…

Him Well?

Amy (*taking courage*) Well, no, actually I'm not, as a matter of fact.

Him Oh—well—too bad then—ain't it? Too bad.

Amy (*quietly*) Yes. I suppose it is.

Him You're bloody marvellous you are. You've always got to piss on the chips haven't you? Here we are nice and cosy an' that … and you've gotta bring up the soddin' past—as if it mattered.

Amy Doesn't it?

Him No—it doesn't, Amy. We're all right. We poodle on from day to day—what's wrong with that?

Amy I see.

Him This is because I'm going away—innit? Just because I'm having a week away?

Amy In Spain.

Him On business, Amy, on business!

Amy With Myra Leadbetter.

Him Myra… Who told you *that*?

Amy Well—it's true.

Him (*always shifting the blame to her*) Never mind whether it's true or not… Who told you?

Amy Is it true or isn't it, Jack?

Him Look—just answer the question—who told you?

Amy I saw the tickets didn't I? Jack? I saw the soddin' tickets—in *her* name! You couldn't even be bothered to hide them could you?

Silence

I suppose one day you'll just go altogether—for good.

Him Oh, here we go… Moan, moan, moan—nag, bleedin' nag—nag.

Amy (*getting up to leave the light*) D'you want chips with the spaghetti—or boiled?

Him (*taking her hand*) Here—don't go off like that.

Amy Like what?

Him With the hump. Like I said—you've always gotta spoil things, Amy.

Amy Well…

Him Well what? I thought you was happy. No?

Amy No, Jack. I'm not bleedin' happy. What is there to be happy about for Christ's sake? You take me for a right prat don't you?

Him I don't. Honest, Ame … it's all in your imagination, girl.

Amy I must have a vivid imagination. You're always saying I'm thick.

Him Look—I wouldn't want to upset you—would I?

Amy Wouldn't you?

Him You know I wouldn't. I just want life to be easy.

Amy (*laughing*) Easy? Oh, yeh, you want it to be easy all right. Easy for you, Jack. What if *I* kept having bits on the side? What then? You'd be up in bleedin' arms you would.

Him (*suspicious*) You haven't—have you?

Amy There you are see.

Him You can pack your bags and get out of here if you have. You're not taking me for a bleedin' fool!

Pause. She looks at Him

Amy Chips or boiled!

The Lights on them fade. A pool of light comes up on Holly and Irene

Holly Oh—good-afternoon.   *enter USR*

Irene Hello.

Holly Miss Tyson? Irene Tyson?

Irene Yes.

Holly My name's Masterson. Holly Masterson?

Irene (*without recognition*) Oh, yes.

Holly I wondered…

Irene Yes?

Holly I wondered… I think you know my decorator.

Irene Oh, Him.

Holly That's right. Him. I believe he's been doing some work for you?

Irene Yes—he has.

Holly Are you satisfied?

Irene Satisfied?

Holly With him. With the work.

Irene Quite satisfied—yes. Why?

Holly It's just that—well—I'm a little worried because he hasn't been home for several days.

Irene Home?

Holly Well, not home exactly, but…

Irene But?

Holly Well—the truth of the matter is that he's been—*staying* with me for some weeks, while he was doing the work.

Irene Ah—I see. I thought for a moment you were his wife.

Holly Oh no—I don't think he has a wife.

Irene He told me that he had. A wife.

Holly Really. He distinctly told me that he hadn't. How curious.

Irene Yes. Seemingly.

Holly Has he been here of late?

Irene Of late? No. Not of late. A fortnight ago he popped round to put up a tile that had fallen off in my kitchen. We had some tea— he fixed the tile—and was gone.

Holly I see.

Irene He told me he was doing some work for a lady who reads the news on the television.

Holly That's me. I read the news on television.

Irene (*without recognition*) I see. How nice. And you are also his landlady.

Holly I suppose you could call me that. Yes. So?

Irene So?

Holly He's not *staying* with you then?

Irene Oh no—he's never actually *stayed* with me. He has taken various other liberties—but he's never actually stayed. I shouldn't like that, Miss——?

Holly (*deep in thought*) Yes...

Irene Perhaps Amy is his wife.

Holly Amy? Amy who?

Irene It's just that on occasion—he has mentioned someone called Amy. Perhaps he's...

Holly With her? I see. Would you...?

Irene No—I'm afraid not. But he's due here soon—in a day or two—to finish off my skirting. If you like I'll tell him you're anxious.

Holly Would you?

Irene (*with a smile*) Of course. What was the name again?

Holly Just say his "landlady" called. Good-afternoon.

Irene Good-afternoon.

Holly leaves the light

Your landlady called...

Him joins Irene in the light

Him Oh yeah?

Irene Yes... I thought it was your wife—for a moment.

Him Oh yeah?

Irene Yes—but it wasn't. She's been wondering where you were ... where you were staying.

Him Yeah?

Irene I said that perhaps you were with your wife—with Amy.

Him Oh.

Irene Perhaps you could start on the bedroom now.

Him I thought I'd give it a go outside today ... the garage doors perhaps... No?

Irene Much too cold for outside work. Leave that until I'm not here, when I'm at school. Much nicer to work inside at weekends—I would have thought.

Him But I've got the paint specially—for the garage doors.
Irene Pale green? As we agreed?

Long pause

Him (*with a smile*) No ... bright blue.

The Lights on them fade. A light comes up on Amy

Amy Life's been smashin' since he came. It really has. I'd never
have thought an odd-job man could make such a difference to a
home. The kids love him—they do—and you know Michelle?
She can't abide being cuddled an' all that ... well—she worships
him. He takes her to the pictures an' that, the zoo of a Saturday,
over to the recreation park when it's sunny ... mind you—it puts
him all behind with the work an' that, but you can't have
everything can you? He's done all my inside passage, my hall, the
well of my staircase ... he's even swept my chimney and I never
expected that! He's a delightful worker—he is—delightful... I
can fully recommend him. I'd never have thought of doing my
kitchen blue ... I mean—blue! But you should see it: very
uncommon.

Holly steps into her light

(*Looking at Holly*) Yes?
Holly (*with a smile*) Amy? You must be Amy.
Amy That's right ... Amy. Don't tell me—I know that face—
here—aren't you...?
Holly That's right.
Amy And don't you...?
Holly Yes—I do... Isn't it a small world. Have you seen *Him* lately?
Amy Him?
Holly Our decorator. Our hanger of wallpaper. Him!
Amy Well ... funny you should ask. He left here about three days
ago ... yes—Thursday it was. He left to buy a tin of blue paint to
put the finishing touches to my kitchen and...

Holly You haven't seen him since?

Amy That's right ... still—I expect he's snowed under—he takes too much on if you ask me. Were you...?

Holly Expecting him home? Yes.

Amy Home? Oh—I see. Home. You mean...?

Holly Yes, I'm afraid I do.

Amy Oh... I say... I thought...

Holly Yes. So do most people. But it isn't so.

Amy You mean ... you and him is...?

Holly That's right.

Amy He's a caution in't he? A right bleedin' caution.

Holly Has he been—*staying* here? On and off?

Amy Well, on the odd occasion—when he was whacked out an' that. Yes.

Holly Oh dear.

Amy I've got a spare room see, in the back—it seemed to make more sense than going home an' that—but I can see now ... I mean ... he never said.

Holly No. Perhaps he wouldn't. It's all very tiresome isn't it?

Amy Well—it won't happen again ... I mean—I shall put my foot down. It isn't on is it? Pity really—because the kids adore him, specially little Michelle... She's grown so attached, over the weeks. Do you have...?

Holly Children? No. Thank heavens.

Amy Well—I don't know what to say really. "Sorry" doesn't seem enough at times like this. Aren't men bastards?

Holly I'm afraid so—yes. Perhaps if you see him before I do you could...

Amy Oh yes, I'll certainly tell him you called—perhaps you could put out an S.O.S ... on the news an' that?

Holly (*coldly*) Good afternoon.

Holly leaves the light

.. To ladder

Amy (*alone in her light*) Here we go ... what a bleedin' life innit?

The Lights on Amy fade

Him takes his place up the ladder and starts "painting"

The Lights come up on Him

Holly comes up and leans at the foot of the ladder

Holly (*reflectively*) It is nice having you here, you know.
Him (*busy painting*) Oh yeah?
Holly I thought I'd become quite independent since Nigel left but
   I shall miss you when you leave.
Him (*still busy*) Yeah…

*Irene takes Holly's place at the other side of the ladder. She is
holding a box of Scrabble*

Irene I thought this evening—when you've finished—we might
   have a game.
Him Oh yeah?
Irene Scrabble that is—if you're not too tired.
Him Right.
Irene I get tired of playing with Cecil—and he's not a very good
   speller. (*She pauses*) He touched my leg the other lunchtime.
Him (*still busy*) Dirty old sod.
Irene I'm sure it was intentional. He pretended it wasn't but one can
   tell… *Death In Venice* is on television tonight.
Him Oh yeah?
Irene Visconti.
Him Yeah, I like him. I'm doing the picture rail in blue you'll
   notice—more striking really.

Amy takes Irene's place

Amy I expect you'll be moving on soon.
Him (*still busy*) Yeah.
Amy I mean you must have nearly finished by now.
Him Right.
Amy You've done every room in the house—from top to bottom—
   you've even swept my chimney which was quite unexpected.

Him All part of the service…

Amy Guess who I met yesterday—getting her veg in Lovall's?

Him Oh yeah…

Amy Muriel Dawlish … she was telling me you'd done a quick job for her last Monday. Dawlish … Muriel…?

Him Yeah—very nice woman.

Amy (*distantly*) Yeah…

The three women freeze

Him You see—it's the same wherever you go. Women—you see 'em right an' that—fix their shelves, clear their drains, paper their ceilings, touch up their garden gates … you know—really put yourself out for their special benefit an' that—and what do you get? Bleedin' aggro … aggro-bleedin'-vation. They want to possess you—hang on like grim death an' that—know what I mean? You lavish them with kindness—and for very little financial recompense—and for what? An' I meet all sorts in my job; school teachers—television news-readers—frustrated house-wives … the lot—and no sooner am I inside that front door than you can see it.

Holly I shall hate it when you leave.

Irene I really have enjoyed you being here…

Amy Little Michelle is going to be heartbroken when you go…

Him See what I mean? I mean—I take pride in my work, nothing shoddy with me. I'm at it from dawn till dusk—I just wanna earn a living an' that—but them! I ask you. Funny really, in't it?

Silence

(*Loudly into space*) Friday. I shall be leaving on Friday.

Holly I'm sorry?

Irene What?

Amy Friday?

Him Yeah—Friday. I'll be finished by Friday. I just need to put a new hinge an' that on the whatnot in the hall, then I'm done. I've enjoyed it really, very nice.

The Lights change

Amy and Irene leave the space

Holly But you can't!

Him Can't what?

Holly Leave. How can you leave?

Him Same way I came in—through the front door… By the way I've touched that up with a bit of clear varnish—makes it shine an' that.

Holly But what will I do?

Him Do?

Holly Who'll attend to the jobs?

Him What about Nige? Nigel? You're always on about him—how you and him was so well suited an' that—what about him?

Holly (*hoping it might work*) He rang the other day.

Him Oh yeah…

Holly Yes, he's not happy with Patricia—it seems they have very little in common.

Him Shame.

Holly He didn't actually say, but I suspect he's begging to come back.

Him Nice. Perhaps he could unblock your outside toilet.

Holly (*knowing it hasn't worked*) I thought you were happy here. I've tried to make everything—comfortable.

Him Oh I've been happy … 'course I've been happy, but it's time to move on—pack my bits and skedaddle—see?

Holly Well—I'm not pleased. I don't think I've had my money's worth … some of the work is substandard.

Him Oh—yeah? Complaining now are we?

Holly That crack in the conservatory ceiling—it's reappeared—the stuff you used wasn't strong enough.

Him Really?

Holly Please don't go … I mean—even if you don't do any more work you can still stay. The little back bedroom is always vacant. I've grown accustomed to your face…

Him Christ—we'll all be singing in a minute By the way—you owe me four hundred quid—for materials an' that.

Holly Materials?

Him Yeah … materials and labour—four hundred. That includes V.A.T. and a new pair of overalls.

Holly Overalls—what is this?

Him The old ones got torn in your washer—see?

Holly Washer—overalls—V.A.T.? I thought we had a long term agreement?

Him Nothing's long term in this world—you should know that— reading the news an' all.

Holly Well I think I'm being treated rather shabbily … extremely shabbily in fact. I've made you so welcome, I've fed you and everything.

Him Too rich, the food has been far too rich. I've got a very delicate stomach see—mustn't touch olive oil … gives me the shits an' that see. I didn't want to say too much in case you took it the wrong way… By the way, I'm taking that tin of blue paint—you'll not be needing that will you?

Holly Blue … but I don't like blue… I hate blue.

Him (*with a smile*) I know. That's why I'm taking it. (*He stares at her with much meaning*) See?

Silence

Holly (*quietly*) Where will you go?

Him (*slowly; deliberately*) Home … to the missus an' that.

Silence. Holly stares at him   Ext USR

Amy comes and joins them

Amy You're going to that news-reader woman I suppose.

Him turns to Amy

Holly walks off

Him Actually… I've finished with her as well—coincidentally I've finished you both at the same time as it were... No—I've got pastures new to attend to—there are other walls crying out for the attention of my brushes ... see?

Amy She's been a bad influence on you ... you say everything as if you were reading the soddin' news.

Him I've finished doing the out-house—I'm sure you'll like it.

Amy I'm sure I shall—thanks.

Him I need only dip the brushes in turps then I'm off... By the way—you owe me four hundred—I'll waive the V.A.T. seeing as how it's you ... a friend an' that.

Amy (*after a pause*) It's her isn't it?

Him I beg your pardon?

Amy Don't be fuckin' "upmarket" with me! I've seen the state of your underpants remember... It's her isn't it? You're going to her.

Him Her?

Amy Muriel Dawlish.

Him She has a lot needs doing, has Mrs Dawlish.

Amy You're telling me.

Him She wants her place entirely refurbished—from top to toe, from cellar to ceiling—and like you she's not handy when it comes to hammer and nails.

Amy Will you stay there?

Him I might—you never know—she's got a comfy little box room with its own little sink an' that ... could be very homely.

Amy stares at him

Irene comes on to join them: she carries Him's coat

Amy So that's it then?

Irene So that's it then?

Him (*turning to Irene*) Yeah ... 'fraid so, Miss Tyson.

Amy walks off

Irene I see. Miss Tyson?

Him Best to be formal when it comes to parting ... what? Saves all the tears and bitterness.

Irene I'm not crying—nor do I feel any bitterness—I've enjoyed having you. (*She blushes*)

Him (*surprisingly embarrassed*) Yeah ... well.

Irene How much do I owe you?

Him Oh ... well ... that's all right. I realize you're not flush an' that...

Irene Oh, no. I wouldn't dream of it.

Him Well—let's say ... sixty quid, eh? How's that? That's fair I think, no?

Irene Oh—very fair—I'm really more than pleased.

Him Fine.

Irene Do you have a base?

Him Sorry?

Irene A number where I can contact you—if I needed some running repairs and ... all that—a base.

Him Oh, well ... not really ... my wife—she don't like phone calls—see... She suffers from an illness that necessitates absolute peace and quiet. It drives her screwy—see—the phone.

Irene Perhaps I might find you at Amy's? Or the lady who reads the news perhaps?

Him No ... no.

Irene watches Him as he puts on his coat and collects his stepladder

Well, it's cheerio then ... Irene.

Irene (*quietly*) Yes.

Him exits with his stepladder

Cross-fade to three separate pools of light   at side—at chair

Amy, Holly and Irene each stand in a separate light

Amy You know what that bastard gone and done? He painted my second toilet bleedin' red! I ask you. Bleedin' red! He was a right take on I can tell you. I couldn't recommend him—in all honesty I could not recommend him—and he wasn't cheap. I can tell you that for nothing ... I think—all in all he cost me well in excess of eight hundred quid ... well—that's not cheap is it? And I'll tell you another thing—he wasn't altogether honest, nothing big mind, just bits and pieces ... tea bags—the odd spoonful of coffee an' that ... but it all mounts up. And I'm a one-parent family now I'm on me own an' that ... and—now I wouldn't say this to anyone else but—well—he was often quite suggestive an' that—you know—suggestive ... well—I mean—I'm independent now—self-sufficient—I'm not into all that any more ... thank God—eh? An' I'll tell you what ... you know that blue paint in my kitchen ... well—it's peeling. No—I couldn't in all fairness recommend him...

Holly Yes, there was a man—just after Nigel left actually—odd sort of fellow really ... strange—you know—he knocked on the door one day and you know me ... naïve to the end ... he looked to be somewhat down on his luck—and what did I do? I let him in didn't I? I know—don't tell me... It's because they know my face you see. I'd feel so guilty turning people away. I just would ... anyway—as it turned out he *was* quite useful. I gave him a cup of tea and he offered to decorate my little conservatory—well, my God! It *did* need a going over, so ... there you are. Nice little man really—you could see he was infatuated—but I get it all the time. Nigel was like that ... and it can be so tiresome—anyway, he came back the next day and the day after that and ... well, between you and I, I don't think he had a decent place to lay his head—but I couldn't have allowed him to stay ... that really would have been too much. (*She pauses*) Yes—TV-am... I have been offered a chat show on Channel West—but—honestly... I'd be terrified!

Irene (*reflectively*) Yes—Dingleworth—near Swanstone Manor ... the Cheviots? Lovely spot... I went back you know... I got a cheap day return ... on the coach from Victoria ... stopped on the motorway for lunch. It was lovely—really—(*her smile fades*) but I wish I hadn't ... it's all changed. They've built a council estate in Pendlecrest, an absolute eyesore. I only went back for old time's sake—but I shouldn't have gone. (*She smiles*) Still—we all do things we regret ... don't we?

A doorbell rings

All three women turn their heads enquiringly To Ladder

Black-out

FURNITURE AND PROPERTY LIST

On stage: Stepladder
          Paintbrush
          4 chairs

Off stage: Glasses, *The Times* (**Him**)
          Box of Scrabble (**Him**)
          Paint-stained overalls (**Him**)
          4 cups of coffee (2 **Amy**, 1 **Irene**, 1 **Holly**)
          Him's coat (**Irene**)

LIGHTING PLOT

Property fittings required: nil
1 interior. The same throughout

To open: Four separate pools of light

Cue 1   **Him**: "…should look nice…"   (Page 13)
        Black-out. Then bring up pool of light round
          stepladder

Cue 2   **Amy**: "Chips or boiled!"   (Page 15)
        Fade pool of lights on ladder. Lights up on **Holly**
          and **Irene**

Cue 3   **Him**: "No … bright blue."   (Page 18)
        Fade lights on **Him** *and* **Irene***. Lights up on* **Amy**

Cue 4   **Amy**: "…life innit?"   (Page 19)
        Fade lights on **Amy**

Cue 5   When ready   (Page 20)
        Lights up on stepladder

Cue 6   **Him**: "…very nice."   (Page 21)
        Change lights

Cue 7   **Him** exits with stepladder   (Page 25)
        Fade all lights except for three separate pools

Cue 8   All three women turn their heads enquiringly   (Page 27)
        Black-out

EFFECTS PLOT

Cue 1　　**Irene**: "…do things we regret … don't we?"　　(Page 27)
　　　　　Doorbell